Kids' Guide to Common Alaska Critters

MW00950307

Here's how to find the animals in this book:

Small Land Mammals

Bat, Lemming, Shrew . . . . Page 1

Arctic Ground Squirrel, Red Squirrel, Flying Squirrel . . . . Page 3

Vole, Weasel . . . . Page 5

Medium Land Mammals

Beaver, Coyote, Fox . . . . Page 7

Lynx, Marmot, Muskrat . . . . Page 9

Porcupine, River Otter, Snowshoe Hare . . . . Page 11

Wolf, Wolverine . . . . Page 13

Large Land Mammals

Black Bear, Brown Bear, Polar Bear . . . . Page 15

Bison, Caribou, Dall Sheep . . . . Page 17

Deer, Elk, Moose . . . . Page 19

Mountain Goat, Musk Ox, Reindeer . . . . Page 21

Marine Mammals

Sea Otter, Walrus, Beluga Whale . . . . Page 23

Bowhead Whale, Humpback Whale, Killer Whale . . . . Page 25

Fish

Halibut, Salmon . . . . Page 27

Insects

Mosquito, No-seeum, White Sox . . . . Page 29

Small Land Mammals
(Mammals are animals that have live babies and feed them milk.)

BAT -- There are many types of bats in Alaska, but the most common is the little brown bat. These are tiny little animals that are less than four inches long and weigh about as much as a nickel. They live in caves, chimneys or attics and are found almost everywhere in Alaska. Like all bats, they sleep in the daytime and fly at night. They make high-pitched sounds while they are flying, and these sounds bounce off solid objects, like sonar, and help the bats find food in the dark. This is called echolocation. These bats eat insects, like mosquitoes and moths. Animals that eat other animals are carnivores.

LEMMING -- Lemmings look a lot like gerbils. They have grayish-brown or brown fur, tiny ears and short tails. There are three kinds of lemmings in Alaska, and two kinds of animals that are called lemmings but aren't. All of them are little and light. They weigh a little bit more than a C battery and usually don't get any longer than about six inches. They eat leaves, seeds, grass, twigs and insects. Animals that eat plants and other animals are called omnivores. Some lemmings cut grass and store it underground to eat during the winter. Foxes, wolves, coyotes, owls, hawks, and other animals eat lemmings. As many as 11 babies can be in one litter, and as many as three litters a year may be born. When there are too many lemmings in one area, some have to migrate, or move away, to find food.

SHREW -- Shrews are the smallest North American mammals. The smallest shrew is about two inches long. The largest is about six inches, but half of that is tail. Shrews may be little, but they have a big appetite. They eat all the time. A shrew can eat its own weight in meat every three hours. (How much would a shrew have to eat if it was as big as you?) They eat insects, worms, spiders, mice, small birds and dead animals, called carrion. If they can't find meat to eat, they will eat plants. Shrews have lots of babies at a time, in litters of up to 10. Babies are about the size of a honey bee. By the time they are four weeks old, they are big enough to hunt for themselves.

1

SQUIRREL -- Squirrels in Alaska include the Arctic ground squirrel, red squirrels and flying squirrels.

Arctic ground squirrels are about the size of guinea pigs. They live almost everywhere in Alaska, except parts of Western and coastal Alaska. They are active in the summer, when food is plentiful. They sleep underground all winter long. This is called hibernation. Babies are born in the spring, in litters of five to 10. They weigh about as much as a nickel when they are born, but by the time they're six weeks old they are ready to go off on their own. They eat seeds, stems, leaves, insects and bird eggs, sometimes stuffing their cheeks until their faces are all puffed out. They are also called parky squirrels because Alaska's Native people sometimes used their fur to decorate parkas.

Red squirrels aren't really red, but sort of rust colored. They have a long bushy tail. When they are sitting, their tail curls up over their backs and necks. When they are running, it streams out behind them. When they are sleeping, it may be curled over their nose and eyes. They eat spruce cones, mushrooms, seeds, berries, and sometimes insects and birds eggs. [*Do you remember what animals that eat both plants and other animals are called? Hint: It starts with an "o".*] Red squirrels store food for the winter. They are active all winter, but stay in their nests when it is very cold or stormy. They live in trees or alder bushes. Babies are born in spring in litters of three to seven.

Flying squirrels don't fly like birds. They don't have wings or feathers. They have folds of skin on their sides between their front and rear legs. When they jump from tree to tree, they stretch out their legs and the skin folds spread open like a kite. They are are light brown to rust on their backs, and cream-color on their stomachs. They are nocturnal, which means they are active mostly at night. They eat all kinds of food including mushrooms, berries, nuts, seeds, eggs and insects. Things that like to eat them include hawks and owls. They have two babies a year, in the summer. The babies are born without fur and with their eyes and ears closed. It takes almost a month for their eyes to open, and about eight months before they look like their parents.

VOLE -- Voles are little hamster-like creatures that live in Alaska's fields and forests. They are less than six inches long when full-grown. There are several kinds of voles in Alaska. The two most common are the meadow vole and the red-backed vole. Meadow voles can eat as much as they weigh every day. They eat seeds, berries, roots and leaves. Animals that eat only plants are called herbivores. Voles are brown or reddish brown. Voles are active all year long, making tunnels and nests under the snow during the winter. Lots of other animals like to eat them, so voles have to watch out for coyotes, foxes, weasels, wolves, owls, hawks, shrikes, dogs and cats. Animals that are hunted by others are called prey

WEASEL -- Weasels are fierce little hunters that live almost everywhere in Alaska, except on some of the islands, such as Kodiak. They are longer than voles, but aren't much wider, and they usually weigh less than half a pound. They are very fast. They can eat almost half as much as they weigh every day. Voles are their favorite food, but they will also eat shrews, birds, insects and, sometimes, fish. [*Do you remember what animals that only eat other animals are called?*] Weasels change color with the season. In the summer, they are brown with a white chest and belly. In the winter, they are all white, except for a black tip on the tail of the short-tailed weasel. Another name for the short-tailed weasel is ermine. Some people trap ermines for their beautiful fur. The other type of weasel in Alaska is the least weasel. It is smaller than the short-tailed weasel, and it hardly has any tail at all.

Note: Words that would be good for you to know are in a shaded box like this. Did you guess that?

Question: Animals that eat only plants are herbivores. Animals that eat only meat are carnivores. Animals that eat both are omnivores. What kind of animal are you?

LYNX -- Lynx look like large, fuzzy, short-tailed cats with big feet. They have long hair, called tufts, on their ears.They are a kind of cat, but they can weigh as much as a two-year-old child. They measure about two feet high at the shoulder and can be more than three feet long.They live in or near forests or brushy areas. They live alone, except when they come together to mate. Also, lynx mothers stay with their babies for about a year. Lynx babies are called kittens. Two to four kittens are born in each litter. Lynx have thick, grayish-beige fur. Their big feet help them stay on top of the snow when they hunt. They hunt for snowshoe hares, or any other animal they can catch. [*Do you remember what an animal that eats other animals is called? Hint: it starts with a "c".*]

MARMOT -- Marmots are furry rodents. Do you remember what a rodent is? Marmots are about the size of a small dog or a large puppy. They have thick fur and look a little like a big ground squirrel. They live in burrows under the ground but spend much of their time above ground gathering food. They eat plants. Marmots like to be around other marmots and often live in colonies, but they are shy with people. When people are near or they sense danger, marmots whistle a loud warning and run to hide. They hibernate, or sleep, all winter long, deep in their burrows. They spend their summers raising young and eating to store fat for their long winter nap. Marmots have two to eight babies a year. There are three kinds of marmots in Alaska: the hoary marmot, the Alaska marmot, and the woodchuck.

MUSKRAT -- Muskrats are large, furry rats that live like beavers. They build lodges next to ponds and swampy areas and they eat plants that grow in and under water. They are smaller than beavers. They usually weigh less than five pounds and their bodies are about as long as a 12-inch ruler. They are brown and they have long, skinny tails. Muskrats have two litters a year and may have eight babies at a time. They live almost everywhere in Alaska, except for the far north.

PORCUPINE -- Porcupines are short, plump animals that have long barbed quills all over their backs and tails. The quills can stick in the mouth and nose of animals that try to bite a porcupine. Porcupines don't see very well and they don't move very fast, so their quills help protect them. Porcupines eat the bark from spruce and birch trees, but they especially like leaves, buds and plants that grow in the water. Porcupines weigh about a pound and are about 10 inches long when they are born. When they are adults, they weigh 15 to 20 pounds and are as long as two 12-inch rulers. They can live as long as 10 years.

OTTER -- Alaska has two kinds of otters: river otters and sea otters. **River otters** live on the land, but they spend a lot of time hunting and playing in rivers and streams. They have webbed feet and are excellent swimmers and divers. They run as fast as a person, and on hard snow or ice can go even faster by combining running and sliding. They have short legs but long bodies, measuring up to 60 inches, or five feet, long. They eat fish and shellfish, insects, birds, and small mammals. Otter mothers can have as many as six babies, or pups, a year, although they usually have only two or three. Pups usually stay with their mothers for about a year. For a description of **sea otters**, see **Marine Mammals**.

SNOWSHOE HARE -- If you saw a snowshoe hare, you would probably call it a rabbit. It looks like a rabbit, but its legs are longer. Snowshoe hares weigh three or four pounds and are about 18 to 20 inches long. In the summer their fur is light brown and white. In the winter, it is mostly white. Snowshoe hares get their name from large furry hind feet that help them to run on the snow. They have four to six babies two to three times a year. Babies weigh two ounces at birth, about as much as a C battery. They are born with fur, and can walk almost as soon as they are born. They start eating greenery before they are two weeks old. Snowshoe hares eat grass, buds, twigs and leaves. Animals that eat snowshoe hares include hawks, owls, foxes, coyotes, lynx and wolves.

WOLF -- Wolves are wild cousins of the dog. They range in packs, headed by two dominant leaders. The leaders are the only ones who breed and have pups. The two next most dominant animals in the pack take over if anything happens to the leaders. All the other animals in the pack have to give in to the leaders. Wolves look a little like German shepherd dogs. They have a long snout, pointed ears, a long, bushy tail, and thick fur. They can be white, although gray or black wolves are most common. Adult wolves weigh 85 to 130 pounds, as much as a small person. Wolves are carnivores and predators. Did you remember that that means they eat meat, and they hunt? Wolves hunt as they live, in packs. In Alaska, they hunt moose, caribou, sheep, snowshoe hares, ground squirrels, voles, and sometimes birds or fish. They will hunt whatever is most available and easiest to catch.

WOLVERINE -- Wolverines are very large members of the weasel family. They weigh up to 35 pounds and measure up to four feet long. They have short legs, though, and may be only 15 inches tall at the shoulder. Baby wolverines, called kits, have white fur when they are born, but by the time they are adults they have long, dark brown fur. On each side of their bodies, a wide light-colored stripe runs from shoulder to tail. People sometimes trap or hunt wolverines for their fur. Wolverines are omnivores, which means they eat just about anything. They especially like to eat snowshoe hares and animals that other predators kill. But they eat whatever they can find, including berries and birds. Wolverines live alone . It is rare to see one in the wild.

Question: Animals that hunt others are predators. Animals that are hunted are prey. Which kind of animal are humans?

14

BEAR --Three kinds of bears live in Alaska: black bears, brown bears, and polar bears. They weigh anywhere from 150 pounds to more than 1,500 pounds -- as much as 150 10-pound sacks of potatoes. When they stand on their hind legs, the biggest bears can be as tall as 10 feet. How tall are you? Bears are active spring through fall, but in the winter most find a cozy den and go to sleep, or hibernate. Male bears are called boars. Females are sows. Babies are cubs. Cubs are born in the winter, while their mothers are sleeping. They weigh only about a pound at birth, less than a human baby, and by spring they have reached 15 pounds. They stay with their mothers for two years, until they are big enough to take care of themselves and go off on their own. Boars don't stay with the females or the cubs, and sometimes will even attack cubs when they see them. But bear mothers are watchful and take good care of their babies. It's a good idea to stay far away from a mother bear with cubs.

Black bears are the smallest bear in Alaska. But they aren't always black. Sometimes they are the color of cinnamon, or brown, or even blue-gray. Some people call the blue-gray bears glacier bears. Black bears weigh from 150 to 400 pounds. They like the forests and climb trees easily. Like people, they are omnivores, which means they eat just about everything, but they especially like berries.

Brown bears are bigger than black bears. They weigh from 400 to 1,500 pounds. Brown bears live about anywhere they want to in Alaska. The largest live in coastal areas and in forests. Other live on the open space called tundra. They all eat whatever they can find, but they especially like parky squirrels, berries, and salmon. Brown bears that have blond or silver-tipped hair are called grizzly bears.

Polar bears and brown bears are related, but they look different and live entirely different kinds of lives. Polar bears are white or yellowish-white, just like the snow and ice where they live. They live along Alaska's far northern coast and out on the ice of the Arctic Ocean. They eat mostly sea creatures, especially seals. They can get to be as big as 1,500 pounds. Unlike most bears, male polar bears do not hibernate.

BISON-- Bison are sometimes called buffalo. They were brought to Alaska in 1928. They live south of Fairbanks in herds of about 50. Some weigh more than 2,000 pounds, or about half as much as a full-size pickup truck. They have big heads and shoulders and look like they are wearing a dark brown, furry cape. Both males and females have horns, although the males' are bigger. Males are called bulls. Females are cows. Babies are calves. They eat grass, mostly, but sometimes they also eat shrubs and twigs.

CARIBOU -- Caribou are members of the deer family that live on the tundra, or wide-open country. They often range in herds of thousands of animals and live in most areas of Alaska. They travel long distances to find food. They eat willow leaves, grasses, small plants, and lichens. They are ungulates, which means they have hooves. They are a little smaller than a horse and a lot smaller than a moose. Males are called bulls and females are cows. Both wear antlers, although the males' antlers are larger. The antlers grow in two directions: up, and out over the forehead. Caribou babies are called calves. They are born in late May or early June and can run with their mothers when they are only a few hours old. Wolves, brown bears and humans hunt caribou for food. Reindeer are domestic, or tame, caribou.

DALL SHEEP -- Dall sheep are the only wild white sheep in the world. They live high in Alaska's mountains. In the summer, they look like clumps of snow on the green grass or gray rocks, but they are hard to see in the winter, because they are the same color as snow. Their hair is hollow, and in the winter, their coat may grow to three inches thick. Both male and female Dall sheep grow horns, but the males' are larger. Their horns grow into a large curve that ends at the side of their faces. Males are rams, females are ewes, and babies are lambs. Rams weigh about as much as a man and ewes weigh as much as a woman.Lambs are born May or June, and weigh about five or six pounds. Usually only one lamb is born at a time, but sometimes a ewe will have twins. Sheep stay together in small flocks. They eat mostly grass and other low-lying plants. Wolves, bears, eagles and humans hunt Dall sheep for food.

DEER -- There are many members of the deer family in Alaska, but only one true deer. The Sitka black-tailed deer lives in the forests along the coast of Southeast Alaska, Prince William Sound, and Kodiak and Afognak Islands. It is much smaller than the other Alaska members of the deer family: moose, caribou and elk. Males, called bucks, usually weigh about 150 pounds, or less than most men. Females, called does, weigh less.These deer are reddish-brown in the summer and dark gray in the winter. Males grow antlers. Does usually have two babies a year. The babies, called fawns, are reddish-brown with white spots. Sitka black-tailed deer eat beach plants, bush tips, and leaves. Wolves, bears and humans eat them.

ELK -- Elk are not native to Alaska. Alaska's herd started with eight elk calves that were brought from Washington to Afognak Island near Kodiak in 1929. By the mid-1960s, there were more than 1,200 elk on the island. In 1986, some elk were taken to Southeast Alaska. Elk are members of the deer family, but they are larger than most deer. They are not as large as moose, though. Males are called bulls, and they grow antlers. Females are does, and babies are calves. Calves are born in spring. Elk eat grass and low-lying plants in the summer, and bushes, roots and mushrooms in the fall and winter.

MOOSE -- Moose are the biggest members of the deer family. When they are born, moose babies weigh about 30 pounds. How much do you weigh? By the time they are adults they can weigh as much as a small truck. Male moose are called bulls and grow big, broad antlers or "racks." Female moose are cows, and babies are calves. Some people think moose look funny. They have big noses, big ears, and a long furry growth under their chins called a bell. But moose are very graceful and can move through thick brush so quietly you don't even know they are there. Most deer live together in herds, but moose stay by themselves most of the year. Calves stay with their mothers for a year, then their mothers make them go off on their own. Moose spend a lot of time eating. They eat plants, leaves, and twigs. They especially like willow leaves and twigs. They also like to eat vegetables out of people's gardens.

MOUNTAIN GOAT -- High up in Alaska's coastal mountains live white, hairy animals with sharp black horns and black hooves. They are mountain goats. They are about the size of sheep, but they have long hair, rather than wool. Both males and females grow horns. Male goats are billies. Females are nannies. Babies are kids. Kids weigh about six pounds when they are born. Adults can weigh up to 350 pounds. Mountain goats can walk easily on steep slopes and rocks where other animals would have trouble. This helps them avoid animals that would like to catch and eat them. They graze on grass and other low-lying plants in the summer. In winter, they browse on twigs and any other plant life they can find.

MUSK OX -- A musk ox looks like a big long-haired block with horns and hooves. [*Do you remember what animals with hooves are called? Hint: It starts with a "u".*] Musk ox hair is so long it almost touches the ground, so Inupiat Eskimos call it "oomingmak." This means "the animal with skin like a beard." Both males and females have horns that grow down from the forehead along the side of the face. Males are called bulls. Females are cows, and babies are calves. Adult bulls are about five feet tall at the shoulder and can weigh as much as a medium-size horse. Babies weigh about 30 pounds when they are born, but by the time they are a year old, they can weigh more than 200 pounds. Musk oxen eat grass, leaves and small woody plants. They live in herds of up to 75 animals. When they feel threatened, the herd forms a circle around the young, with their horns pointing out. There are few wild musk ox herds in Alaska, but people can see musk oxen at the Anchorage zoo and musk ox farms in Fairbanks or Palmer.

REINDEER -- Reindeer are domestic caribou. They were imported, or brought, to Alaska from northern Europe in the 1890s. Some people thought it would be a good idea for Eskimos to learn to herd them. Some people did herd them, but most Eskimos continued to hunt for seal, walrus, whale and caribou. There are still some reindeer herds in Alaska.

22

Marine Mammals
(Marine mammals live in the sea, but must breathe air, just as you and I do.)

SEA OTTER -- Sea otters live in the ocean, usually near the coast. Some people call them "Old Man of the Sea," because of their bristly white whiskers. They spend a lot of time floating on their backs, resting, or eating. They eat fish and shellfish, including clams and sea urchins. They dive for their food, then bring it back to the surface of the ocean where they use their chests as a table. Sometimes they'll bring up a rock, too, which they use to break shellfish. Sea otters have one pup every one or two years. Pups weigh less than five pounds when they are born and can weigh as much as 100 pounds, or a small person, when full grown. Grown sea otters are about as tall as 12-inch ruler, but they are as long as four rulers. Sea otters don't have a lot of body fat, so they rely on their soft, thick fur to keep them warm in the cold sea.

WALRUS -- Walruses live in the water off Alaska's west and north coasts. They are as big as some small cars, and they have two long tusks, or teeth, sticking straight down out of their mouths. Male walruses are called bulls. Females are cows, and babies are calves. Babies weigh more than 100 pounds when they are born. (How much did you weigh when you were born?) Walruses eat food they find on the bottom of the ocean, including clams, snails, crabs, shrimps, and worms. Eskimos hunt walruses for their meat, skins, and tusks. The tusks are ivory, and Eskimo artists carve them into jewelry and other art objects.

WHALE -- There are two types of whales, toothed and baleen, and 15 species of whales in Alaska waters. Here are some of them.

Beluga whales are small, white, toothed whales. They grow to 16 feet long. That sounds long, but most whales are much longer. Belugas swim in groups called pods. They eat fish, and are often seen chasing salmon and other fish along the coast of Alaska. Some people call belugas canaries of the sea, because of the chirping noise they make underwater. Male whales are called bulls. Females are cows, and babies are calves. Calves are born live, like human babies, but in the sea.

Marine Mammals

Bowhead whales are baleen whales. Instead of teeth, baleen whales have a series of fringed plates in their mouths that filter plankton, or tiny marine life, from the water. They can grow to more than 60 feet long and they can weigh more than 60 tons, or as much as 12 African elephants. Bowhead whales are an important species for the Inupiat Eskimos that live along Alaska's northwest coast. The people who live in the villages along the northern Bering Sea and the Arctic Ocean are allowed to hunt a few bowhead whales each year for food. Whalers from many countries, including the United States, used to hunt whales for their oil. Now, only a few nations still hunt whales. Eskimos hunt whales mostly for their meat and for their blubber. Blubber is a layer of fat that keeps whales warm, even in the coldest water.

Humpback whales are baleen whales found all along the Alaska coast south of the Bering Sea in spring and summer months. People see them in the waters of Glacier Bay, in Southeast Alaska, where they come to feed. Sometimes the whale catches plankton, called krill, and small fish by blowing a tunnel of bubbles around it. Then the whale swims up inside the tunnel with its mouth open, gobbling up all the tiny animals inside. Some people call humpback whales singers of the sea, because they make up songs and sing them wherever they go. The songs change every year, but humpback whales all over the world sing the same songs the same year. Humpback songs don't sound like our songs. They sound like a series of grunts, groans and wails. But if you play humpback songs at a fast speed on a tape machine, they sound just like a bird's trill. Humpback whales are about the same size as bowhead whales.

Killer whales, or orcas, are toothed whales that eat other sea mammals and fish. They are beautiful black and white whales with large triangle-shaped fins on their backs. They live, and sometimes hunt, in groups called pods. They are about about half as long as a bowhead whale and only weigh as much as 2 elephants. Newborn baby killer whales are almost half as long as their mothers and can swim as soon as they are born. They can live as long as 40 years.

Fish

HALIBUT -- Halibut are flat fish that live on the bottom of the ocean. When they are born, they have eyes on either side of their heads, like most fish. As they grow, their eyes move and by the time they are adults, both eyes are on the side that is on top. Halibut are gray on top and white on the bottom. The older halibut get, the bigger they get. They can be as big as 10 feet long and weigh more than 400 pounds, but most are smaller. The biggest halibut are females. Some people call the big halibut barn doors. Many people like to fish for halibut, because its meat tastes very good.

SALMON -- Salmon are fish that are born in fresh water, spend their lives at sea, and then come back to fresh water to spawn, or lay their eggs. Pacific salmon die after they spawn, unlike Atlantic salmon, which can spawn again and again. Five species of Pacific salmon swim in Alaska waters. These are coho or silver salmon, king or chinook salmon, sockeye or red salmon, pink or humpback salmon, and chum or dog salmon. King salmon are the largest. They sometimes weigh as much as a small person, or 100 pounds. Some people say that chum or dog salmon got their nickname because people used to catch them to feed to their sled dogs. Other people say they got the name because when they spawn their mouths look a little like a dog's mouth. Alaska fishermen catch millions of salmon each year for people to eat.

Question: Fish live in the water and get their oxygen right from the water. They also lay eggs, which later turn into tiny fish. How are marine mammals different?

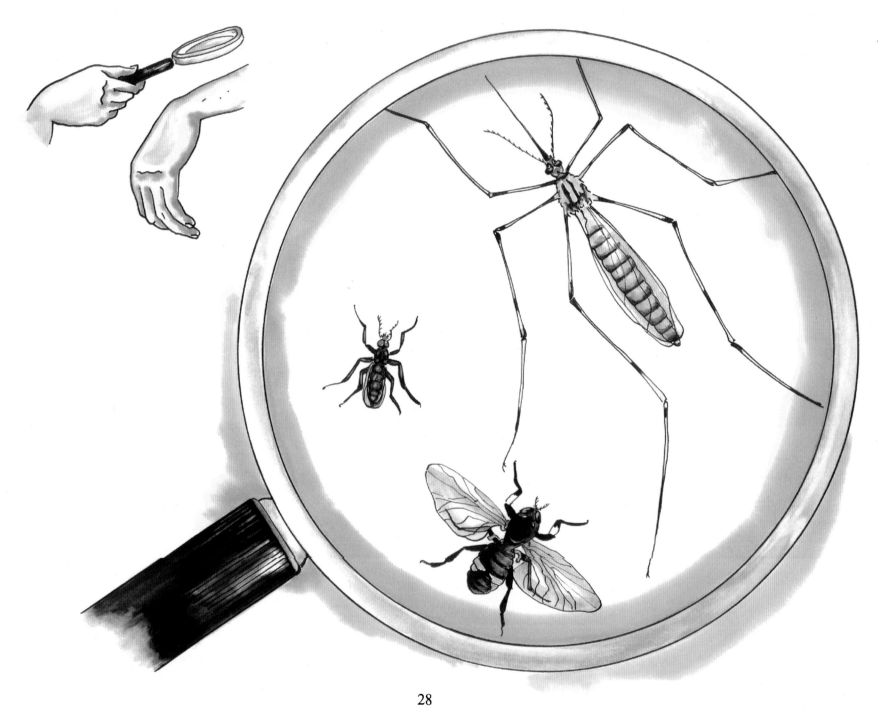

Insects

MOSQUITO -- Mosquitoes are small winged insects that have a big bite. Actually, they don't bite, but poke long, needle-like suckers through an animal's skin. Female mosquitoes need blood to lay eggs. They will suck blood from any warm-blooded animal, including people, to get it. Mosquito bites usually turn red and itch. Mosquitoes lay their eggs in still water. Alaska has lots of lakes, ponds, and puddles in the summer, so it has lots of mosquitoes. People use mosquito repellant to shoo mosquitoes away, but other animals can't do that, so often they will try to find someplace windy to stand. Mosquitoes are so light that a breeze can blow them away. Fish like to eat the mosquito babies. Some birds like to eat the adults. There are at least 27 different species of mosquitoes in Alaska.

NO-SEEUMS -- These are tiny little flies that bite. If you feel a sharp bite, but you can't see what bit you, chances are it was a no-seeum. They are active in summer. No-seeum bites often get red and itch, and sometimes look like a rash. No-seeums are also called punkies. They are so hungry, they'll even bite mosquitoes. They lay their eggs along lake and river shores and in beach tidal areas.

WHITE SOCKS -- White socks are tiny flies that bite. They are black, but their feet are white. Did you guess that? They are active in summer, mostly in woods, swamps, and along the water's edge. They lay their eggs in fast-moving streams, and, like mosquitoes, need blood to lay eggs. They are sometimes called hunkies or buffalo gnats.

Here's a reminder of what the adults and babies of various species are called:

Males	Females	Babies
Billy -- Mountain Goat	Nanny -- Mountain Goat	Kid -- Mountain Goat
Boar -- Bear	Sow -- Bear	Cub -- Bear
Buck -- Deer	Doe -- Deer	Fawn -- Deer
Bull -- Bison Caribou Elk Moose Musk Ox Walrus Whale	Cow -- Bison Caribou Elk Moose Musk Ox Walrus Whale	Calf -- Bison Caribou Elk Moose Musk Ox Walrus Whale
Dog -- Fox	Vixen -- Fox	Kit -- Fox Beaver Wolverine
Ram -- Dall Sheep	Ewe -- Dall Sheep	Pup -- Coyote Otter Wolf
		Kitten -- Lynx